THE
GIFTED

*How to live the life
of your dreams*

DAPHNE MICHAELS

DAPHNE
MICHAELS
BOOKS

The Gifted: How to Live the Life of Your Dreams
©2014 Daphne Michaels

All rights reserved. No part of this document may be reproduced
in any form or by any means, electronic or mechanical, including
photocopying, recording, or by any information storage and
retrieval system, without permission in writing from the publisher.

Note to the reader:
This book is not intended as a substitute for the medical advice of
physicians or for mental health diagnosis or treatment. The reader
should regularly consult a physician or mental health professional
in matters relating to his/her health and wellbeing and particu-
larly with respect to any symptoms that may require professional
diagnosis, therapeutic attention or treatment.

Daphne Michaels Books
621 Pacific Avenue
Tacoma, Washington 98402
www.daphnemichaels.com

ISBN: 978-0-9914689-0-4

DAPHNE
MICHAELS
BOOKS

For me there is only the traveling on paths that have heart, on any path that may have heart, and the only worthwhile challenge is to traverse its full length — and there I travel looking, looking breathlessly.

- Carlos Castaneda

Contents

Author's Preface

When I was very young, and life was turbulent – as it often is for the young – I had an experience, call it a vision, that showed me two vast, human worlds in terrible contrast: One of love and one of despair. I couldn't reconcile these worlds and was tortured by my failure. Human beings could choose to live in either world, and yet so often they chose the world of despair almost exclusively. Why? And who was I, a girl of nineteen, driving to a mountaintop to escape her terrible vision, to think she could figure out what our long human history of strife and suffering had not resolved: How to live with love for oneself and others, and, by doing so, achieve a beautiful and completely satisfying life – the kind human beings dream of.

But shouldn't I, in my life (that teenager asked herself), try to understand how such different worlds could exist both within us and without? To understand how to acknowledge both? To find the secret to bringing heaven and earth together for an authentic, permanent human happiness and, in turn, an exhilarating life? Shouldn't I at least *try*?

I had no choice but to try, though I did not know it at the time. That is the way of all life callings, isn't it? All I knew as I drove down the mountain was that I had been changed by the stars that particular night. I had been given insights I could not yet name, and they would guide me – even if it took years – to realizing the kind of beauty in life that can only come from reconciling those two all-too-human worlds.

That mountaintop decision never left me. It drove my life's work and over the years led me to understand that there are gifts – nine of them, in fact – that we are all born with but rarely experience in their full glory and potential. These gifts – which make each and every one of us "The Gifted" of this book's title – are the keys to living lives of endless possibilities and, in turn, achieving an authentic happiness that cannot be lost. They are, in other words, the keys to achieving the life of our dreams.

It is these nine gifts that I have joyfully, tenaciously and lovingly celebrated with the wonderful, committed women and men I have worked with at my institute over the years. It is to these nine gifts that the book you're holding – the first in a series about how "gifted" we all truly are – is dedicated. It is my hope that in understanding the power of these gifts you will see how to use them to transform your own life, and, by doing so, discover the eternal joy of embracing at last the amazing person you are.

THE GIFTED

How to live the life of your dreams

– One –

The Gift of Awareness

The most beautiful thing we can experience is the mysterious. It is the source of all true art and science. He to whom this emotion is a stranger, who can no longer pause to wonder and stand rapt in awe, is as good as dead: his eyes are closed.

- Albert Einstein

Life's greatest mystery is inside us. It is inside every living thing. Like the deep secrets of the universe, the mystery inside us will never be fully explained. By exploring it, however, we can discover gifts available to us that can change our lives forever.

Life's great mystery is *awareness*. More basic than thoughts and more primal than instincts, awareness does not require a centralized brain, as scientists have proven through studies with invertebrates like starfish. While these beautiful creatures have no centralized brains, they possess *awareness*. Starfish, like all invertebrates, use awareness to perceive, eat, grow, reproduce, and survive.

Awareness is so intrinsic to life that it defines life: living *means* being aware. From the beginning of life – before we take an initial breath – humans demonstrate tremendous awareness. Prenatal psychologists have discovered that we experience, while still in our mother's womb, not only light and sound but, even more astonishingly, *emotion*. We kick our legs when agitated by loud noises and sway pleasantly to beautiful classical music. Months before birth we grimace at the taste of sour amniotic fluid and drink heartily when it is sweet. Awareness grows as we grow.

As we develop as human beings, our awareness stretches in all directions – from awareness of our five basic senses to awareness of external events around us, from awareness of our emotions to awareness of our thoughts, from limited awareness of a topic that bores us to an expanded awareness of topics we feel passionate about. Of all the many dimensions of awareness, the highest form is *self-awareness*. With self-awareness we begin to appreciate just how far awareness actually extends. Just as ocean waters are deeper than the surface of the sea, awareness is deeper than the surface of our physical body or our conscious thoughts. The infinite depth and breadth of awareness is filled with gifts that are ours to receive.

Our Most Valuable Resource

At a time when the entire world seems to be spinning out of control, understanding that awareness is our most valuable and practical personal resource is crucial. Rather than having us search high and low for answers to life's problems in the same old places, awareness takes us beyond what we already know into realms of endless discovery: Realms where rebirth *always* follows destruction. Realms where new horizons continually appear in sight. Realms where new solutions inevitably come from our sheer willingness to delve deeper into an invisible resource that is always there and can never be depleted.

When we realize that awareness is our most valuable and practical personal resource, we become confident that we can overcome any challenges keeping us from living the life we've always wanted. Through awareness, hope is guaranteed us. The secret to living the life of our dreams begins with understanding that awareness plays a central, crucial role in both the life we're living now and the one we wish to live.

Increasing Our Awareness

Increasing our awareness is not about discovering answers by asking questions in the usual way. Awareness is more organic than thinking. We can only access it through a deeper connection with the self. And we can only achieve that connection through a special kind of relaxation: not the kind of relaxation that puts us to sleep, but the kind that wakes us up.

Like gymnasts on balance beams, we increase our aware-ness through a relaxation that calls forth alertness and focus. Relaxed, alert and focused, gymnasts connect to deeper parts of themselves where awareness exists. If they *think*, they will fall. And when they come off the balance beam, they bring back a special quality to their daily lives.

Self-Guiding Our Awareness

Like gymnasts, we need to come off the balance beam to dis-cover that the gifts we receive from awareness extend farther than we can imagine – into every aspect of our lives. When gymnasts carry their physical strength and mental precision into daily life, their confidence and achievements multiply, bringing even greater success.

Like gymnasts dedicated to developing strength and skill for their sport, we must be dedicated to developing strength and skill in *self-guiding our awareness*. If we are, we will experi-ence deep awareness even when only a moment's opportunity is available, and then come off the balance beam of that moment with gifts that multiply through the ways we live and love.

Self-guiding our awareness means tuning it – from a

lower awareness felt as cloudy or negative to a higher awareness where we live with a constant sense of possibility. We tune our awareness through the state of our very being – in other words, through the state of our spirit, mind, heart, physical body and dreaming capacity. Being relaxed, alert and focused on all levels tunes our being to the most profound awareness possible, one where pure potential exists. In turn, self-guiding our awareness through tuning our being allows us to bring that potential into every aspect of our lives.

Think of the flight control panel in the cockpit of a high performance aircraft like a Learjet. The panel has all sorts of dials and switches that must be perfectly adjusted for flight. The instrument panel has been carefully designed to keep the sophisticated and complex aircraft functioning.

Humans are even more sophisticated and complex. We, too, however, have instrument panels that have been carefully designed, and we must learn to adjust the state of our being through those panels. Our own dials and switches allow us to tune the Learjet of our life to realms of potential impossible to reach through the physical world. Through our instrument panel we can tune ourselves to an awareness that will show us with astonishing clarity how to face the challenges and opportunities of our lives.

Our Inner and Outer Life

Through awareness we discover an amazing truth: that our inner and outer lives are a continuous stream, and so much so that we cannot separate the two. We discover that our life begins in a place deeper than our cells, a place where pure awareness exists. From this place of pure awareness our life streams through countless layers of our inner being, just as an old-fashioned movie projector's light shines through film. Our story plays out on the screen of our life, but it has already been written and etched into the film's frames. Some of the frames we inherited. Some we invented. Some we should have discarded, but didn't. Some we hold for the future. Some we hold for others. Some we enjoy seeing played on the screen of our lives, while others we wish we could have cut out of the production altogether. But by the time we realize that our inner and outer life is one continuous stream, our movie is already playing in theaters. We directed it, and we were, we realize, asleep.

We may try hopelessly to change the movie of our life as it plays on the screen. We may stand up in the theater and stick our hands in the flow of light. We may jump up and down screaming that we hate the movie. We may cause such commotion that the movie no longer makes sense to us or anyone else watching it. We may deny that the movie is our life and swear that someone who didn't really know us wrote the script. We may storm out of the theater; but as we stomp up the aisle trying to contain our dismay, we see our wiser self in the projector room waving, trying to get our attention. Our wiser self is shouting: "The movie playing is *interactive*! While you can't stop it from rolling, you can dramatically change it through *awareness*!"

Interacting With Our Life's Movie

When we learn to tune the state of our being so that we are both deeply connected to our inner self and fully engaged in life, we live as though we are the gymnast on the balance beam, but are not limited by its narrow margin of space. We are completely free to move about in our life however we choose as long as we remain aware. We are flexible, relaxed, strong, clear, focused; and we are able to think, feel and engage life at its highest potential. We live and love creatively, and the gifts we receive multiply exponentially. Our awareness makes everything we touch a gift to ourselves and others.

Every thought we have is a gift; every word we speak is a gift; every idea we consider is a gift. Through awareness we realize that life itself is a gift and that the movie of our life is indeed interactive. We realize that everything is connected to everything else, and that interacting with life's movie can bring enormous changes in amazingly brief periods of time.

Through awareness an entire landscape of potential will appear before us. Life will never be the same again. We will realize we have been blessed with an incredible opportunity to live the life of our dreams – and the only question is "Will I answer – with sincerity and commitment – opportunity's knock?"

– Two –

The Gift of Potential

*My theology, briefly, is that the universe
was dictated but not signed.*

                    - Christopher Morley

P*otential* is both everything and nothing at the same time. For this reason the idea of potential can be deceptive if we don't approach it with real understanding and respect. It is natural to want "potential" in our lives; but unless we understand what potential really is and how to carry it into our lives, we will misuse the idea of it.

How many times have you witnessed dreams dissolve into nothingness because the notion of "potential" was taken too lightly? We have all banked on potential that never became a reality because we didn't do what was necessary to make it a reality. Perhaps we did not receive promotions, opportunities, dividends, or love because we took the idea of potential too lightly. We quit our jobs and moved out of town feeling certain we would find better work in another location; but we didn't treat the transition seriously enough – with the respect it deserved – and the potential slipped away. Or we left good relationships (ones with real potential) betting that better relationships were within our reach; but, rather than finding that amazing new partner, we ended up doing exactly what we thought our true soul mate was doing: waiting for the connection to happen. When two people just wait for one another – no matter how much potential there might be in their union – nothing happens.

Ignoring potential creates sorrow for ourselves and others. How many frantic parents live through nightmares when their children don't take their own potential seriously and the parents don't know how to help them? We've all witnessed – and in many cases lived – scenes of parents dragging their children by the scruff of their necks toward their potential while sensing that this can't possibly be the best way to do it. We experience the same frustration with friends, other family members, spouses, and even ourselves when we just don't know how to approach potential.

There is good news, however. We can indeed gain the knowledge we need in order to embrace potential respectfully and effectively. Through *awareness* we can, if we are committed to it, begin to see potential not superficially, in a glib way, but as an inner resource surging with the power to make our life's movie a thrilling, epic and completely satisfying adventure. When we discover how to direct our potential throughout the layers of our being, we will find a new way to breathe, think and feel – and, by navigating potential effectively, create the lives we are meant to live.

Choice

When you think of *choice*, what do you feel? Most people feel a river of contradictory currents – a mix of fear and excitement. A part of us wants to reach for *choice* – to feel our fingers touch the dial of choice on the instrument panel of our Learjet. But another part of us fears that as soon as we turn the dial of choice, we will regret it. Perhaps we fear that someone is going to be unhappy with our choice. Perhaps we turn the dial of choice to please others, and we're unhappy with ourselves for doing so. When we engage our deepest potential, however, we learn something amazing about choice: that when we exercise positive choice from a deeper part of us – the part where awareness and potential reside – we create a force that brings something new and special to our lives.

Choosing – that is, turning the dial of choice in a direction we know is right for us – is always life-changing. When we look back at positive crossroads in our lives, we often recognize that we made our choices from a sense of deeper potential. No one else could have made the decision for us. We needed to make the decision ourselves. Our potential catalyzed our positive choices, allowing them to fund our life for years to come.

Unfolding in Gratitude

Plants *unfold* from seeds, and they vary greatly depending on what they receive in water, nutrients, sunlight and other environmental factors. Two seeds that may look identical can produce plants significantly different in size, shape, strength and ability to produce. The most breathtaking flowers come from seeds saturated with elements that support growth.

Our own lives unfold from the deepest part of us. They, too, must be saturated with elements that support growth. Safety, love and support are elements that help foster our potential and thereby support our capacity to create the lives we've always dreamed of.

One element that can greatly nurture our potential, but that we often overlook, may be the most promising of all. It is *gratitude*. Gratitude fosters joy, and joy frees our potential, in turn creating gratitude. Through gratitude we appreciate not only what we have in life, but who we truly are, and we appreciate it at the depth of our being. We appreciate others for both who they are now and (if they are taking their own potential seriously) for who they are becoming. By cherishing the people we hold close, the places we enjoy, and the life we have yet to experience, we fill our deepest selves with gratitude. When we combine it with other elements that support growth, our lives will naturally, powerfully and in celebration unfold from their greatest potential.

Transformation and Surrender

As we begin to nurture the unfolding of our potential and the cultivation of sincere gratitude, we may discover that past choices have given us a life we now – in our greater awareness – find unacceptable. We feel damned if we do and damned if we don't. We may be unhappy at work, but we worry that getting a new job in the same industry may not make us happy. We may feel that our relationship with our partner in life isn't healthy and that we need to do something about it, but we also know that band-aids won't work. At such times, when we recognize that little changes won't fix what's really wrong with our life, we may feel hopeless. But through *transformation* we will discover that we have the capacity not just to change part of our life, but to transform it all. The dial of transformation on our instrument panel, however, can seem impossible to turn. In trying hard to turn it, we make an important discovery: that to turn the dial of transformation we must first flip the switch of *surrender*.

When the starfish is young, it is so small and unformed that we can barely observe it. It lives close to the surface of the sea. This is its way of life – swimming near the surface, eating, growing and preparing to sink eventually to the bottom, where it will become a crawling "sea star." To transform itself, it must surrender to nature – to a natural process that is deeper and wiser and more powerful than it is. If it fights to remain near the surface, it cannot become what it is meant to be.

There are times when we need to transform. We may need to leave behind a career, a marriage, a community, or an entire way of life. To enter such a dramatic metamorphosis of life and self, we must sink to the depth of our own being – to an awareness that is deeper and wiser and more powerful than simple consciousness. If we fight to stay on the surface, we will never become what we are meant to be. When we emerge from that metamorphosis, our lives will be entirely different. Even if it doesn't seem so to others at first, our transformation will be apparent not only in what we are leaving behind but in what we are bringing forward into our lives from the depths of ourselves.

Self-Sufficiency

There is no greater way to attain *self-sufficiency* in our lives than learning to navigate the world with a sense of our own deep potential. As we learn to follow our potential more, we will gain self-confidence and eliminate the external obstacles that have held us back from the life of our dreams. When we stop seeking permission or approval from others, we discover – in the kind of epiphany and miracle that real awareness provides – that we never really needed external forms of acceptance to live our life fully. Even when we feel stuck in our lives – trapped by our salary, our body image, our age, our sense of isolation, our past choices that haunt us – any despair we feel will vanish the instant we truly connect to our potential.

The world may wield enormous power, but so do we – just like that Learjet. When it dawns on us at last who we really are, and how interactive the movie of our life truly is, we will awaken to a rebalancing of power between our inner and outer lives. That rebalancing will be as enormous as the shifting tectonic plates of an earthquake. Once the plates settle, we will discover *stillness* and, in that stillness, stand before the universe as we never have before.

– Three –

The Gift of Stillness

With all your science can you tell how it is, and whence it is, that light comes into the soul?

- Henry David Thoreau

Awareness and *potential* reside in our being like a shining two-sided coin. The coin is there in our pocket; it is valuable. We may have forgotten it. We may be saving it for a special day. To exchange the shining coin for something we want in life, we must reach for it and, as we do – in the millisecond before touching it – discover *stillness*.

Sometimes we feel a hole inside us we cannot fill. We describe it as feeling lost, broken, famished or desperate to find something we cannot name. We try everything to rid ourselves of the never-ending pain inside our hearts and guts, but nothing we try works. Relationships, success, spending, eating or even intoxication can't distract us from the pain, or numb it, or obliterate it – at least not for very long. Nothing can take our pain away... until we find stillness.

Stillness is the open space that holds the shining two-sided coin of awareness and potential in the depths of our being. Discovering stillness is always a life-changing experience. Stillness not only heals our suffering, but propels us toward the life of our dreams. Through stillness we find our true foundation – that authentic ground to build our life from. It is our source of creativity and genius, for, as research has shown, there is "genius" in us all if we can only access it.

A Shared Foundation

Stillness is a state we can all reach and cultivate. It is available to each of us and at every moment if we simply pursue it. Not only is it a deeply personal experience, it is also the *shared foundation* that unites us with all other human beings. Cultivating stillness and knowing that we can all reach it at any time produces benefits beyond imagining. Our awareness and potential demand stillness. Knowing this can also help us understand that we are both unique individuals and a part of a larger, vibrant whole in which isolation is illusion.

Just as modern physics teaches us that light can be described as both particle and wave, stillness teaches us that we can know ourselves both as individuals and as a part of the human universe. What we have felt as "isolation" and its suffering suddenly becomes a powerful sense of union, one in which we see at last that the lines separating us into cultural, religious, gender, age, political and geographical camps are insignificant.

Rest

Much has been said over the past few decades about the cost of personal exhaustion in our society. "How rested am I really?" is a question we should ask ourselves when we have difficulty coping with stress. While there are many factors that contribute to fatigue, *rest* will always be a major ingredient in the cure. Resting – not only during sleep, but also while we're awake – gives us an edge in life. Developing a habit of accessing stillness during the day can provide us with a quality of rest beyond the merely physical. It brings a sense of renewal to everything we are: mind, body and spirit.

Resting in stillness feels like floating. The weight of our body and the weight of our problems suspend, giving us an opportunity to reach the awareness and potential that lie in the depth of our being. By resting in stillness we can truly discover the gifts inside us waiting to be claimed.

Creative Impulse

Stillness allows creativity. It fosters the *creative impulse* that can ignite deeper awareness and greater potential and, in turn, give birth to something entirely new in our lives, changing us within and without.

How many times have we heard others talk about ideas that came to them out of the blue, and how, if only they'd acted on them, they'd be rich now? "I had an idea. I don't know where it came from. I should have acted on it because now someone else has, and they've made a fortune!"

Creative impulse is often experienced "out of the blue." When it is, it has arisen from stillness. Each of us expresses creative impulse in a unique way. Even the idea that someone else has made a fortune on – one that sounds so similar to ours – is unique. It isn't exactly like our idea at all, for creative ideas are unique, arising from the individual. They are distinct and wonderful because they are.

To what purpose will we summon and channel our creative impulse? Will we create expressions of beauty or pain? If we choose to express pain, what is our actual intention in doing so? Is it to aid healing and forgiveness, or is it to perpetuate negativity?

With creativity comes responsibility. The power of creative impulse traveling through just one individual has the potential to change history, as we have seen time and time again with artists, philosophers, statesmen, athletes and reformers.

Those who use their talents simply to live the right way – the way "truest" to them – affect the entire world. Whether we express our creativity in intimate circles of family and friends or through media-celebrated public deeds, we express it from the same impulse. And creativity is something we all put to use, whether we know it or not, each and every moment of our lives.

Genius

Genius is a word full of mystery. Genius has been defined as everything from a spirit to a special talent in the arts or sciences, and from exceptional intelligence to an individual man or woman of achievement. It's as if genius cannot be reduced to a single definition, as if it were too grand and mysterious to be captured by the human mind. This shouldn't be surprising. The genius inside us all is real and powerful, and it works its magic better if we don't try to pigeonhole it.

Genius may appear as a novel solution to a problem, a shift in paradigm that frees us, a new way of relating to loved ones, or even a new way of simply *being*. Genius often appears with a shock of recognition: "Wow! That is brilliant!" Its power can transform our entire thought process in a split second, and it often leaves us with a smile, a tear, or even the glow of ecstasy.

To accept the genius within us we need to greet it with joyful anticipation. Sometimes we wake in the middle of the night with thoughts so brilliant we're amazed, but then fail to take action to remember our exceptional thoughts. We simply return to sleep and wake later to a hazy memory of what might have unfolded in our lives for years to come, changing everything, had we let it.

When we realize that genius, like creativity, comes from *stillness*, we understand that genius is both something we are born with and something we must develop. While we may be immersed in stillness when we are born, we need to develop our gifts of genius in daily life. We need to respect and remember our brilliant moments of "Aha!" and "Eureka!" and *unfold* them in our lives, turning them around in our mind and polishing them like precious gems. The ultimate catalyst for genius comes from honoring the genius within, from using it in our own lives and offering it to others for theirs.

Healing

Life is filled with mixed messages about *healing*. On the one hand we are undeniably responsible for our own recovery from illness or disease. On the other, we must arrange over time a personal team of professionals who can help us maintain health. While we may have many options in healthcare, *stillness* offers an important instrument in our healing. Because it is not external to us, it is one no professional can provide. Headaches, chronic pain, depression, fatigue, addictions and many other ailments improve and even resolve through stillness. While stillness is not a form of medical treatment, our capacity to heal increases the moment we discover stillness at the depth of our being.

Not only can stillness affect observable healing, it can improve our general, ongoing health through what might be called "micro-healing." Micro-healing is the moment-by-moment process of tiny, continuous, health-ensuring "corrections" to our mind, body and spirit. When we cultivate stillness, we invite continuous healing in our lives for both ourselves and everyone around us.

Inspiration

Of the many gifts of stillness, *inspiration* is one of the most dramatic. When we live by inspiration, we are living life powered by stillness. In stillness we are supported by the heartbeat of nature and the echoes of time. Stillness is not only the foundation we share with one another now, it is the same foundation that has unified the universe from the very beginning. Just as we drink the same water that our ancestors drank – because all water on the planet is recycled forever – when we connect to the depth of our being, we touch the same stillness that has always been there.

We visit the ocean's beaches for inspiration. We climb to the tops of mountains to find it. We search for it through every art form, every relationship, every job and mission. We must remember, though, that inspiration is waiting inside us to be claimed; that, while external things may trigger it and help us claim it, it is indeed ours for the claiming even without such external triggers. Through stillness we can taste the sweetness of eternity and infinity, all of creation, and our own personal essence in a single resonant breath, and claim an inspiration that will allow us to live life to its fullest.

Grandeur

Stillness offers us the gifts of creativity, genius, healing, and inspiration. If we float without navigation, intention and goals, however, we cannot fully use these gifts. Rivers of stillness must run strongly enough through our being to meet the challenges of daily life. Those rivers are grand and epic, and we must keep this in mind when daily life feels like an onslaught of mundane trivia and distractions or negative forces greater than ourselves. We must hold onto the epic *grandeur* of those currents of stillness when we feel too small or insignificant to face, strong and proud, our challenges. The grandeur of stillness will remind us that we have the capacity beyond measure to transform the constricted architectures of our lives. The grandeur of stillness will, in fact – by letting us access the essential triad of *awareness*, *potential* and *stillness* – allow us to navigate against all odds and even see as a gift the most challenging realm known to humanity: the realm of *disharmony*.

– Four –

The Gift of Disharmony

In the dark time, the eye begins to see.
- Theodore Roethke

*A*wareness, *potential* and *stillness* are like water: They cannot be created or destroyed. Just as our cells are filled with water, we are born filled with awareness, potential and stillness. They are our birthrights; they come with life itself. They are not provided by others, and they cannot be taken away. They will always be a part of us even if we sometimes forget this.

People often ask, "Why is my life – and the world around me – filled with such *disharmony*?" The question carries angst, suffering and general unhappiness, and the woman or man asking it has little expectation of receiving an answer that might remedy that unhappiness. Yet there is an answer that can and will remedy it.

We often feel that disharmony will always dominate our lives. We believe we simply need to learn how to cope with disharmony and accept the misery it carries. We're told that life is about suffering, and we can only do our best to make it through. Joy is a foreign concept, and, because it is, the notion of living the life of our dreams makes no sense to us –

until we learn that disharmony in life is a gift, too, one that can teach us what is real and what is illusion.

Discovering why our lives and the world around us seem filled with disharmony leads us to recognize and realize endless possibilities for a completely satisfying life. By understanding how disharmony is created in the first place, we can move from joyless lives to a confidence that lets us pilot our own personal Learjet to higher altitudes of satisfaction. We can learn to steer up and away from disharmony.

To understand why disharmony dominates humanity and how to navigate our lives above it, we must understand how the human ego functions. The term "ego" has been tossed back and forth between Eastern spiritual teachers and Western psychologists so often that we're often confused about what it means. "I have been told by my spiritual teacher that I need to let go of my ego, but my therapist says I need to strengthen it in order to cope better with life." Such confusion prevents our seeing an important secret to life: Professional behavioral analysts and spiritual sophisticates aren't the only ones who can understand "ego"; nor should they be. Understanding "ego" in its context within us is crucial for us all. It is, in fact, a key to navigating and piloting that wonderful Learjet of our life.

Let us change the analogy for a moment. Imagine a garden hose. At one end it's connected to a faucet on a beautiful piece of land covered with grass. At its other end lies a large community garden. Many other hoses reach from the water source to the community garden. Each hose provides water, and all will share in the garden's harvest. While every hose is unique, it carries the same water. The most important variable in how the water is delivered to the garden can be found in the nozzle.

Each nozzle is the interface between the water located deep in the earth and the garden. The water reaches the garden through the nozzle. For this reason the nozzle – even though it is a small part of the entire water delivery system – can bless or doom the garden. What if the nozzle has been crushed or is clogged with dirt and can't deliver the amount of water it should? What if it is corroded, and the corrosion is toxic to plants? What if it is at a setting so harsh it will kill plants? But what, instead, if the nozzle is newer, kept clean, and at the right setting, so that it delivers the water it should and in a fashion right for the garden, thereby nurturing it? Would this better nozzle be an inspiration or a threat to the community?

In this analogy, the nozzle is the human ego and the garden

is society – what we often think of (especially with the help of news media) as the mundane, chaotic and very negative world around us. Eastern spiritual teachers have long encouraged students to let go of the ego because, just as the nozzle of the garden hose may limit the flow of water, the human ego limits *awareness*, *potential* and *stillness*. From the perspective of the nozzle, the task – which may feel daunting – is to water the garden. From the perspective of the spiritual teacher the task is instead to back away from the garden to see the splendor of nature, to follow the water hose back to the faucet, to its source of water deep in the earth. This vision of the universe nourishes us in more than just physical ways. Advanced spiritual teachers encourage us, in fact, to follow the water underground and thereby discover an entirely new dimension of awareness, potential and stillness within us and without.

From a Western perspective, our concern, however, is the garden: How will we bring water to the community and grow a thriving society for everyone – ourselves included? From this perspective, we should encourage the strengthening of the ego so that it can carry more water to the garden and produce a robust harvest.

In the mundane, chaotic and often negative world around us, the focus becomes the nozzle. We become obsessed with how the nozzle can be improved, thinking this is how to make the garden yield a more robust harvest. We reward the hose possessing the better nozzle by giving it a greater return from the garden. We wrongly assume that a strong, perfect nozzle must be developed. Bigger, better, brighter, decorated, and styled for the season, the nozzle becomes the focus – too much so. Context has been lost. Nozzle – and ego – becomes everything. Soon the question of whether or not the nozzle is producing water (its physical function) becomes secondary to its "image": Does the nozzle in question *look* like it can produce a lot of water (whether it can or not)? Does it appear bigger, fancier, more impressive," better" and therefore more important than other nozzles? Function gives way to the brightest feathers. Competition rages for the best-looking nozzle – new and therefore better – and soon the harvest is forgotten in favor of a garden full of neurotic, competitive, posturing, self-important nozzles rather than ones who might carry best the nourishment of plants for society's sake. The garden and the nozzles set up to serve it become a "quagmire," that is, a place of disharmony. All nozzles view this quagmire as "the one and only world," one that cannot be escaped. Like the ego, the nozzles in this insane garden feel they must control the game and beat the competition.

They operate by fear and the need to control. When they can't control and win the greatest share of the garden, they feel miserable. What a silly scenario, but this is how the ego prefers to live. Why? Because of *fear*.

Fear

A life lived with only a dribble of awareness, potential and stillness is inevitably filled with *fear* and the disharmony that comes from fear. When many lives produce such dribbles, they create an entire society of fear and disharmony. Fear is the absence of the confidence needed to face the challenges of life. When we use only limited parts of our entire being – not the vast water supply deep within us – we sense rightly that we cannot access the power to face those challenges, and our confidence suffers. Fear keeps us in a hyper-alert mode and makes us act from impulse rather than wisdom. Fear undermines our ability to evolve as human beings, in turn making it impossible for us to rise above the quagmire. The ego is the source of fear, and, with it, the countless mental and emotional states that make for epidemic suffering in the world.

Entitlement

Where we're afraid, we feel the universe is set against us. We have no power. When we feel powerless, we demand to be taken care of. We feel entitled. In other words, when our egos feel threatened by the quagmire, *entitlement* becomes the ego's strategy: "I must have my share of the harvest," the ego screams, "or I will die!" Puffing itself up to accomplish its self-centered, fear-based goal, the entitled ego connives to take as much as possible from the garden. It takes for itself because it is afraid. Yet it often does so in the righteous name of family, race, gender or a self it sees as "victimized"– whatever will justify its taking while keeping the world from seeing its fear. It stockpiles, too, for the future, because the future is a scary place. But no matter how much the ego takes, it is never satisfied because the taking cannot make the fear go away. An entitled ego is a fearful one and must have more and more and more.

Perfectionism

Perfectionism is another of the ego's sad, fear-based conditions. When we're driven by perfectionism, we live in a constant state of anxiety. Our stomachs are tied in knots because we believe that, if we're perfect, we will constantly receive from the garden what we need...and no longer be afraid. The community garden promises, as ego sees it, to harvest many kinds of "food" – money, possessions, companionship, hope, power, "the good life," self-esteem – but all of these, to the ego, merely represent safety, a place where it does not need to be afraid. When we're perfectionists, we work our fingers to the bone trying to get ahead, trying to be perfect, trying to have what the quagmire promises but does not deliver, and trying to be loved – by others and ourselves. Instead, we become unhappy versions of what we truly are, driven by a terrible sense of longing and a fear-driven need to *do*, and *keep doing* – until we're *perfect*. We deny the fear within us by trying for a perfection that is not only impossible but completely unnecessary, and therefore is doomed to fail.

Shame

When we carry *shame* within us, we are weaker at our cores than we know. Shame is a heavy weight. It is self-attack and burden. It both drains and misdirects our life's energy. It is deeper and more terrible than guilt and not (though we may think so) related to bad choices. Even when we try to cover it with a smile, our shame is often visible to others in our eyes and in how we carry our bodies. In shame, we feel guilty simply for being alive. We don't feel worthy of being. Perhaps we weren't wanted as babies; perhaps we weren't parented later with love and affirmation; perhaps we grew up in physical deprivation, hating ourselves later for it. But shame is not the same as the situations that produced it; shame is what we make of those situations *inside us*. Countless conditions from infancy on – emotional as well as physical – can incubate shame. Once shame is created and becomes part of our ego's identity, it is difficult to rid ourselves of it. The ego sees the community garden as a quagmire, a place of fear. Shame is something to be kept secret for the simple reason that the garden, as the ego sees it, is interested only in how the nozzle looks, not how it feels deep inside, at its core. Only by keeping its shame a secret – even if that means failing to nurture both itself and the garden – can the ego parade as a nozzle "good enough" to be loved and avoid feeling shame.

Self-Doubt

Self-doubt is another disabling condition born of the ego. Self-doubt is a constant, loud "No!" shouted by the ego to our very being. Like shame, it is a terrible weight. It makes living, truly living, impossible. When we carry self-doubt, we have let ego convince us that self-doubt is justified, that there is solid evidence and reason for our feeling it. In self-doubt, as in shame, we cannot access the essential triad of *awareness*, *potential* and *stillness*. We have either lost or never developed a solid and authentic connection to ourselves, one that ensures a trust both in ourselves and in the universe and, in turn, a confidence we fully deserve so that we might live the life of our dreams. In self-doubt, we cannot find a center within our own being to guide the direction of our lives. We constantly second-guess ourselves. We find decisions nearly impossible to make; and when we make them, we toss and turn day and night worrying whether we've made the right ones. In self-doubt we spend most of our life's energy traveling in circles through our own minds and emotions. We rehearse with anxiety, replay with self-recrimination, and make new decisions we think will "correct" the bad ones, though they never seem to. In this terrible and unnecessary struggle with ourselves, we cannot possibly win. We certainly cannot get ahead in life if we remain in self-doubt's loop. We are not truly available for the community garden or ourselves.

Dominance

In its fear, our egos see the community garden as a frightening place, a quagmire full of competing egos just like us. As a result, our egos must control the quagmire and the other egos in it. To control, they must dominate – because anything less than *dominance*, our egos believe, is a weakness and cannot provide safety in the quagmire. If fearful ego can experience dominance by kicking the family dog, it will kick the poor dog. If it can feel dominance by undermining others in the workplace, it will do that. If ego can dominate by cheating thousands of customers or investors out of millions, it will do that, too. Only dominance, our terrified egos believe, can keep the quagmire and the other dominance-seeking egos in it at bay – which of course, in its claim to victimhood and entitlement, it feels it has a right to do.

We witness extreme dominance in the news daily: another child abused, another woman assaulted, another member of a minority group killed, another village destroyed, another group silenced, another individual imprisoned for her or his beliefs, another lawmaker exposed for corruption, a country's domestic or foreign actions driven by desire, and the fear behind it, to control....

Dominance is not always as visible as overt aggression. Passive-aggressive calculations and moves, whether conscious or unconscious, are just as destructive to the heart and soul of a community, to the garden, and to the self as overt aggression is. Silence, withholding, hypocrisy and partial truths can doom the garden to being a quagmire run by egos. When we are only egos – when we are not living fully because we are not being all we really are – we hurt society and ourselves more than we can possibly know.

Imprisonment

We experience *imprisonment*, whether we know it or not, when our egos rule us. It is a prison difficult to escape, its walls reinforced through the habit of negative thinking. When we're trapped in negative thinking, we cannot see a way out of the quagmire because we cannot *think* our way out. Why? Because negative thinking is a loop. It is even an addiction for many. It feeds itself; it confirms its own lens; it sees only what it wants to see. It cannot possibly provide us with the tools we need to break out of it, and so it perpetuates the prison that, on behalf of our egos, it has made for us.

When we are trapped in negative thinking, we aren't able to consider constructive suggestions. We respond negatively to every suggestion. We immediately imagine why possible solutions won't work in our case, and we are intent on making everyone around us agree that we are trapped, that life cannot provide us with happiness, that nothing can possibly change no matter what we do. This habit of negative thinking keeps us imprisoned in joylessness. We don't care about the garden. Why would we? Any action we might take to nourish the garden or ourselves is, we believe, meaningless. All action, in fact, is hopeless. All we can do is protect ourselves from disappointment through our negative thinking. When we are imprisoned in this way by our egos, our vision is so narrow that real *understanding* of the universe and our very real power in it eludes us.

Understanding

Most of us, seeing all the nozzles calling attention to themselves, assume we must become the same kind of nozzle – one driven by our fears rather than a deeper commitment to providing the water the community garden needs for everyone's sake, including ours. Because we see the garden as a quagmire, with competing nozzles striving for dominance and safety, we assume we must live the same way. When we do, we not only contribute to the quagmire, but risk inhabiting it forever and thereby never discovering our true potential to live the life of our dreams.

We can free ourselves from the disharmony in life – from the quagmire – only by real *understanding*, that is, by understanding that such disharmony (and the fear that drives its many faces) is created by ego. Only through understanding that ego imposes smoke and mirrors into the movie of our life, keeping us from creating the life we want, can we choose to live by the essential triad of *awareness*, *potential* and *stillness*. This magical triad is ours by birthright if we will only accept it.

– Five –

The Gift of Harmony

Ten thousand flowers in spring, the moon in autumn, a cool breeze in summer, snow in winter. If your mind isn't clouded by unnecessary things, this is the best season of your life.

- Wu Men

Harmony – as in the phrase "peace and harmony" – is a child of the essential triad. And while we will never escape the prison of the ego without achieving harmony, harmony also has a whispered caveat for us: *If you strive for harmony as an every-second-of-every-day way of life, you will deplete your life's energy and fail.*

We may want to believe that harmony can and should be sustained unflaggingly in life, but it cannot be. Somewhere in the world skies do darken and ill winds do brew. Harmony, like life itself, demands adjustments. If we want harmony to be the entire answer to the problem of the ego, we must forsake the community garden altogether. We must detach totally and forever from it. But can we survive without the garden? Is there any hope for a thriving society without community? In this we face a serious dilemma: If we choose the garden without tending to our own harmony, ego's fear will rage without limit. In the darkest shadows of the quagmire, tragedy reigns. Crimes of passion, suicides, mass shootings, perversity, genocide – all are rooted in egos driven by anguish and their own lack of harmony.

When we face this dilemma – namely, that while harmony is essential to solving the problem of the ego, it cannot be sustained ceaselessly – we will feel three things: (1) An urgency to appreciate the gifts of harmony when we do experience it. (2) A hunch that maybe, just maybe, harmony can provide our Learjet with a super-fuel that will take us from the quagmire to dimensions where the garden can thrive. (3) An intuition that the super-fuel we need can be found somewhere beyond the quagmire of life in a sanctuary both within us and without – one blessed by *awareness*, *potential* and *stillness*.

To find this sanctuary, we realize, we must seek it by intention, not passive expectation. We must set aside time from the demands of daily living to discover the internal and external contentment of harmony and bring it back with us to our busy lives. Only in this way can we thrive despite the pull of the quagmire. We understand that what harmony offers is *gifts* – not entitlements – and that these must be cherished, respected and used for the greater good of ourselves and the garden.

Harmonious environments and activities allow our ego, no longer afraid, to relax. They allow us to let go of perfectionism, shame and self-doubt so that these do not grow like weeds in the quagmire that fear-driven egos have made of the community garden. Spending time with friends in love and support, enjoying the beauty of nature, being a member of a spiritual community, slipping away for a weekend of simple fun, even reading an artful book or watching an uplifting film – these are the kinds of things that bring harmony to our lives and make for sanctuary within and without.

Pleasure

Pleasure is a neurochemical boost to our souls that harmonious environments and activities provide. Often, when we feel there is something wrong with us, and it isn't simply fatigue or illness, we are pleasure-deprived. Human beings deserve pleasure, but fear often keeps us from it. All we need to do to receive the gift of pleasure is get back to riding horses, crocheting a sweater, cooking special meals, swimming, laughing at funny films, climbing mountains, making art, or having rambunctious fun with friends – that is, give ourselves permission to do what brings us pleasure.

When we try to live without pleasure, the result is no

laughing matter. At the same time, pleasure sought by the ego, not from a place of harmony, is short-lived and has unintended consequences: toxic relationships, addictions, serious consequences of all kinds. Pleasure must be sought for its role in harmony. Otherwise, it is false pleasure and cannot serve us in achieving the life of our dreams.

Care

Children who are well cared for – treated with respect and adoration – sparkle like jewels. They glow with self-esteem and seem to manifest what they want and need through personal charisma. Parents, teachers and mentors bend over backwards to open doors for such children because these children inspire in all of us a joy in the present and a hope for the future.

Care – respect and adoration – follows harmonious environments and activities. When we spend time in harmony, we immerse ourselves in care. When we live in harmony, we sparkle like those charismatic children with vitality and self-esteem because our emotional and spiritual needs are met. We inevitably inspire others through the personal charisma harmony provides us with. We inspire them, in fact, to seek their own harmony and its gifts. We are *caring* for them as well.

Openness

The "challenges of life" – the ones in the quagmire the ego has made of the community garden – inevitably harden us. We become closed, guarded, cynical and pessimistic. Our ego toughens, feeling it must run everything. When we are closed to life this way, we overuse the word "No." When we consistently say "No" to life itself, we become withdrawn, shrivel and make for ourselves a sad and lonely life that weighs heavily on the spirits of those around us as well.

Harmony, on the other hand, opens us up to life. As our egos relax in harmony, we become curious again, inspired, and free of "No." *Openness* makes us affirm life with a "Yes!" that is finely tuned to what can and will fulfill us as human beings. Put simply, openness allows us truly to evolve. With our minds and hearts open to new ways of thinking and feeling, we adapt quickly to life's ever-changing circum-stances by carrying both a general good will and a clear and confident analysis of what life offers us. We ask ourselves,

"When meeting the challenges of my life, what positive outcome can I achieve?" In harmony's openness we can consider a wider range of options for resolving any and every challenge we face.

Trust

Harmonious environments and activities cultivate *trust* in our lives. A powerful antidote to weariness, trust rises from harmony. It eases suffering and invites optimism. Of all the children of harmony, trust is perhaps the most valuable. It anchors the center of our being. With trust, a feeling of emptiness is magically transformed into an exciting awareness of our potential.

When we lack trust in ourselves and the universe, we repeat patterns of trauma and disappointment. Life becomes a vicious cycle of expecting the worst and getting exactly what we expect. We put what little trust we do feel into the wrong people and places and are left heart-broken when that trust is betrayed. Then we turn our sense of betrayal into a distrust of trust itself: Fearful ego now tells us we must never rely on anything or anyone else, for they will all fail us.

When we blame trust itself for our problems, we don't realize how we traumatize ourselves. We don't understand that trust is our birthright, central to our very being and central to our ability to live life fully. When we distrust trust itself, we turn on the universe and on ourselves. Everything – including us – becomes the enemy and a terrible weight to be carried, one that makes the life we truly want impossible.

Equilibrium

Emergency rooms are packed with people thrown off balance by the stresses of life. Panic attacks and other stress-related conditions send even the powerful running for help. We all want help managing our fight-or-flight responses to perceived threats from the quagmire. If harmony could be manufactured as medication, it would of course be *the* primary treatment for stress. The *equilibrium* that harmony offers provides the balance we need to live a life of high performance. It ensures stability. It ensures greater confidence in our ability to fulfill life's responsibilities. And it ensures an openness to life, a stance we must adopt toward the universe if we are to begin accepting our gifts.

Courage

Courage – the ability to persevere even in the face of fear – is a child of harmony, too, coming from a place much deeper than mere action or reaction to outer events. It is to be found below the ego's fears and defenses, and it allows us to push our dreams toward reality. By pursuing harmonious environments and activities, we allow ourselves into the depths of our being where courage dwells.

Courage blossoms like buds in springtime, fed by harmony. The greater and more frequent the experience of harmony, the larger and more numerous the blooms. The more buds, the more spontaneously courageous we become. Excited to try new things, meet new people and develop new goals, we begin to live as though the world were a grand ballroom ... and we, dancers eager to step onto the dance floor and dancing to one new song after another.

– *Six* –

The Gift of Ease

Where shall you seek beauty, and how shall you find her unless she herself be your way and your guide?

- Kahlil Gibran

Listening to harmony's whispered wisdom – that struggling to live every moment in sanctuary can only drain life's energy from us – is the first step to discovering *ease*. Ease lets us experience a jet stream in life and proves to us that life can be the exhilarating adventure we've always hoped it would be.

While harmony provides much of what we need for the life of our dreams, it cannot do everything. We must experience ease if we're to be free for adventure and growth – that is, if we're to see risk not from the lens of fear, but as possibility and promise, and live fully with the flow of life's energy.

What sets a Learjet apart from an ordinary airplane is more than its sleek design and outstanding performance. The Learjet's distinctive signature is its creative and skillful expression of elegant avionics. While the first plane designs focused on powerful engines and pilot control, the Learjet based its design on an entirely new concept: the *business rocket*. With its powerful and light *ease*, the Learjet captured the imagination of people around the world and also served them well.

When we begin to pilot the Learjet of our life, we discover an ease that is stylish and beautiful, yet also productive and effective.

When we live with a sense of adventure and the ease that allows it, we capture the imagination of those around us. Even when the odds are against us, we prove to ourselves and others that it isn't what is happening *to* us that determines our happiness and success; but instead how we navigate each and every moment of our lives. And to navigate well we must use the gifts we've been given, ease among them.

When people first experience the exhilaration of ease, they often describe it, not surprisingly, as being "reborn." Everything around them is suddenly fresh and new. They approach life itself with excitement and an eagerness to accomplish what is truly important to them. They pursue their goals with a captivating nimbleness of spirit and reach those goals with much less effort than they could have imagined.

Ascent

Ascent – the rise to a new level – surprises us at first. Carried by life's energy, we discover in ease a velocity and flow that lifts us away from the negative thoughts and emotions weighing us down in the quagmire. Rather than accepting the illusion that we must change our circumstances (and the quagmire with it), we ascend directly to the jet stream of ease and there find new, empowering ways to meet the challenges and opportunities of our lives.

The Learjet's takeoff, like the takeoff of any plane, requires a "runway" – a clear and dedicated ground for its launch. Regardless of the interactions inside the jet between passengers and pilot or the pilot and air-traffic controllers or the pilot and the ground crew, flight is impossible without a runway. The development of our own foundation, that runway, is crucial to our "ascent," and this foundation must come from the essential triad of awareness, potential and stillness. With such a foundation we are ready to become the miracles of flight we need to take off, ascend and soar.

Pressure

Since we're human, we often hear ourselves complaining about the "pressures of life" and announcing that we must somehow get out from under them. We mean, of course, the kinds of pressure – real or imagined – that weigh us down, limit us, make us less than we are, and leave us unable to pursue the life of our dreams. There are good kinds of *pressure*, too, and we must learn to invoke them and use them.

The natural momentum of life carries with it its own "pressure" – an exhilarating current of energy that influences everything we do. This positive pressure requires that we not hesitate in life; that we seize moments of opportunity when they appear and live each day as close to our "best self" as possible. We can and must use this kind of pressure to navigate and shape the life we desire. Our task is to ascend above the disharmony in the world, but our task is also to ascend above the human tendency toward passive harmony, one that waits for things to happen. At higher altitudes, free of the drag of the quagmire and such passivity, the natural pressure of life's momentum becomes the very engine we need to power a new life.

Belief

Ease – that is, our flowing with the natural momentum of an exhilarating life – is like living in an alternate universe, but one that is even more real than the one we imagine (thanks to ego's exhortations) we're saddled with. In this wonderful alternate universe, life's rules change radically. Wonderful things happen so frequently that at first, thanks to ego's voice, we meet them with suspicion and disbelief.

When we first inhabit ease, discovering not only its exhilaration but the ways it seems to affect our lives, we find ourselves starting conversations with "I just can't believe...." We go on to tell stories about job opportunities that seem to have come out of nowhere, relationships that have miraculously improved, illnesses that have somehow healed, little things that have fixed themselves (or "attracted" those who can fix them), and a general sense of well-being and heightened awareness that no drug could possibly provide – or provide for long without a downside.

Like harmony, ease cannot be a constant in life, nor should it be if we're to grow. But the gains we achieve from the times we inhabit the jet stream of ease can last forever as investments in the lives we are designing.

At times, of course, the quagmire of negativity will inevitably drag us back to its game. But a deep and elevated faith in ease – a faith that ease will return again because, once we have visited it, we cannot lose the ability to visit it again – is all we need to pass through the quagmire each time it drags us back. *Belief* in ease, and therefore faith in it, allows us to monitor the current of the jet stream even from below. If we are committed to living a completely satisfying life, we will always find our way back to the jet stream. Each time we do, we will discover we are further along than we were before. Even the quagmire, then, helps us reach the life of our dreams. Our belief in ease protects us from the quagmire's darkness – from all those shouting egos and the havoc they make.

Determination and Elegance

A special kind of *determination* allows us to glide in the jet stream of ease for longer and longer periods of time. Like skaters who love the ice that carries them forward and are determined to excel regardless of the difficulty, we forge this determination from love, too – from a *love of life* and a *strength of will*. When we use both, we achieve yet another state: *elegance*. A determination born of strength of will and love of life is not brute strength; it carries the sophistication and grace of elegance. Left to brute strength, we would slog forever through the quagmire trying to force our way through and making little progress toward the life we dream of. When our determination is expressed through elegance – through that posture of sophistication and grace – we can pull free of the dramas of the quagmire and soar above them.

In fact, our decision to rise above the quagmire of negativity both within us and without ensures elegance as our primary approach to life. Those in the quagmire cannot move with this kind of elegance because the quagmire demands that they live by attack, defense, grievance, feelings of powerlessness, longing, a victim's mindset, and a rough-neck ego-jockeying. This elegance demonstrates by its very posture toward the world and life – its confidence, strength, love of life and refusal to be dragged down into the quagmire – a tremendous respect not only for others, but also for ourselves. When we commit to marrying strength of will to love of life for this elegance, we discover a surprise: We are able to attract much more of what we want and what is essential to the life we wish to live than we ever could before. From the smiles and nods of acquaintances and strangers to opportunities we'd never imagined possible, our determination now miraculously delivers what we truly want in life.

Direction and Imagination

Once we discover how monumental the flow of life is – in that jet stream of ease – we must determine our *direction*, make sure it is the right one, and make adjustments accordingly. Without a clear sense of direction, we will fall out of the jet stream and tumble aimlessly. Having lost the protections of ease, we will be unable to move toward the life of our dreams.

When we're asked what we want from life, we often can't answer the question. We've focused for so long on what we *don't* want – or on external things we believe, in our longing to be happy, will save us – that even thinking about what we truly, profoundly want from life is foreign to us. We are terrified to consider our deepest desires, and are for two reasons: (1) The ego doesn't, in its preference for the quagmire, want us to discover the greater truths and power within us. (2) We doubt that we have such truths and power inside us and don't want to be disappointed by what we might discover there instead. In other words, we have lost the ability to imagine what's actually in us and to access it because ego insists it is fantasy and cannot help us in the "real" world – a world where fear, control, defense and attack are the game rules.

Our direction in life must come from our *imagination*, but an imagination of a special kind: an ability to envision *something truly new*. While a child's imagination may be too big for the practical world, the adult imagination is usually too small. Longings and lotto tickets – fantasies of being saved from our lives and from ourselves – cannot work. We will not reach our dreams through fantasy because what we've fantasized isn't really what we want and need; and yet we must "imagine" a direction true to us in *awareness, potential* and *stillness*. Only then – in the jet stream that lets us see what's really possible in life – can we move forward to the lives of our dreams.

Acceleration

The jet stream alters our experience of time and brings with it a sense of *acceleration* to daily life. Without the essential triad of awareness, potential and stillness, however, we run the risk of traveling too fast and losing the people who are most important to us. At the same time, if we remain connected to the depth of our being, that acceleration can give us the energy we need to realize our dreams. We must use it wisely, then, balancing its gift with the elements of our old life we wish to remain connected to because these parts, too, are essential to our new life.

With acceleration, our appetite for adventure – our desire for "felt passion" and our interest in new things – comes alive. We have the power and velocity to take our life by storm, and our intentions declare themselves. We begin to see a pattern in our life – a story that has been trying to write itself if we would only see it. In the jet stream of ease we now see how to connect the dots over the decades we have lived, and we realize suddenly that our deepest intentions have been at play all along. We may have worked against them in the past, choosing ego's whispers and the quagmire's pull over them. But we see more clearly now. Aware suddenly of how quickly time is speeding by, we understand that we have no time to waste. Every moment counts. But the ticking clock isn't one of fear. It is one of joy, possibility, hope and the promise of a life we have always wanted for ourselves beyond the quagmire's illusions.

Achievements

Our *achievements* in the world define us not only to the world, but also to ourselves. From small accomplishments to major milestones, our personal and professional achievements reflect who we are not only in the world's "résumé" sense, but also in how those achievements have been reached, how they've been lived, and what values lie behind them. When we allow the momentum of life – and the gifts it holds for us – to carry us toward our goals, success becomes part of our daily lives. Through ease, we simply lean in the direction of our dreams and find more success than we could ever have hoped for. We begin to see that each accomplishment is a stepping stone to more and greater achievements and, in turn, to the extraordinary life we are designing for ourselves.

Though we may think we desire success, we are often afraid of it because at some level it makes us feel out of control. Ego, in its fear, does need to feel in control. When achievements begin to accumulate in that jet stream of ease, we may put on the brakes, slow ourselves down in an attempt to manage that subtle fear of success and how that success might change us. We may become distracted by little things or big things, as ego resists. We may even feel we've lost interest in our dreams. But if we listen to ego and stop achieving the things that are truly important to us, we will fall back into the quagmire of negativity.

Through our achievements we discover our place in the world – a place that allows us to live from our true connection to the essential triad of awareness, potential and stillness. We discover a place, both within and without, that gives us the capacity to ascend, over and over again, into the jet stream of ease and there continually discover new heights.

– Seven –

The Gift of Clarity

In the kingdom of glass everything is transparent, and there is no place to hide a dark heart.

- Vera Nazarian

Clarity – that is, seeing the quagmire for what it is and our lives for what they might be – ushers into our life both creativity and the joy that comes from it. Clarity, creativity and such joy are too powerful for the quagmire and, because they are real and not illusions, help us soar above its negativity to the jet stream of ease. Sometimes their magic works quickly, sometimes slowly. But their power to change our lives is inevitable.

Loyalty

We must maintain *loyalty* to clarity. If we claim a desire for greater insight, but turn our backs on what it shows us, clarity becomes even more elusive. We cannot achieve the life of our dreams this way. We cannot achieve it by negotiation or compromise with the quagmire – by trying to remain in its negativity and beating it at its own game. The ego may claim that the quagmire is real and must be attended to, that we must remain in it for others or for ourselves, but its claims are false. It doesn't wish what is best for us, but only what keeps it from being afraid. The ego does not have the special kind of courage that living fully takes. We must be willing to leave the quagmire for good if we're to commit to the essential triad of awareness, potential and stillness and inhabit the jet stream of ease.

When we are loyal to clarity, we pay attention to what is true for us every day. We seek our own deepest awareness, learn from it, and, most importantly, live by it. We make hard decisions based on what clarity reveals, even if it means letting go of what we thought we wanted but now realize we can't or shouldn't have.

When we force our lives into designs, whether those designs are best for us or not, we might as well be trying to force Cinderella's shoe onto her stepsister's foot. When we stop struggling like this, we reach a turning point, a breakthrough. When we accept the fact that some things – a relationship, a job or any way of living that isn't right for us – just won't fit what we want from life, we can discover what really does fit. When we stop forcing our lives to be what we *think* they should be, clarity, creativity and the joy that comes from them will take us back to the jet stream of ease where our potential can bloom once more.

Seeing

Sometimes, despite our intentions and resolve, clarity remains elusive. We may need help sorting through what we don't understand or just can't accept. We want to understand the real nature of our challenges, so that we know best how to meet them, but how do we see clearly what we need to see? If we have the right people to help us, of course we can achieve this *seeing*. But what if we don't? If we have only ourselves, we have enough, it turns out. We can indeed teach ourselves to be our own mentors by persistence and patience. Even when we have the help of others, we must still train ourselves to be our own guides.

Whether it is with the help of others or by our own solo work, seeing the solutions to our life dilemmas, as well as seeing clearly the dilemmas themselves, may take days, or months, or even years. How long it takes does not matter. The instant we commit – that is, the instant we express to the universe and ourselves our intention to live life fully – we begin to change and, with us, life itself changes. We need only remain committed to the journey even when ego (as it often will) whispers discouragement. In this way we will discover how to gain the distance we need to see our life's circumstances clearly.

Knowing

When we stand in inner stillness to watch the continuous stream of our lives – both the way we live inside ourselves and the external circumstances we have helped create – a deep awareness begins to guide our daily lives. That awareness provides a special kind of *knowing* – a kind of instinct that will keep us on track by allowing us to discern the path we must follow away from the quagmire.

Disaster research shows that human beings, when faced with serious physical and psychological challenges, exhibit "altered states" of awareness in which the five senses (and perhaps more) feed the brain's intelligence to create a kind of knowing and problem-solving we just don't experience during an ordinary day. For those living through a disaster, time slows down, they report; everything is bright and detailed; the universe is strangely still; they are truly aware of the physical world, and they do what needs to be done to survive and help others do the same. In addition to experiencing these altered states, people in such circumstances create what psychologists call "therapeutic communities." Everyone helps, joining in for the common good. They have never felt more alive, more attuned to the world. When the threat disappears, they return to their ordinary psychological states. From that time on, they remember the disaster as "the most meaningful time" in their lives. Some even remark, "It's as if I woke up at last – as if, in my life before it and since, I was only sleeping."

Committing through our inner gifts to making for ourselves a completely satisfying life is not the same as a disaster. Physical threat does not drive us. Fear is not the medium that brings us together with others. We, too, cooperate with others, and we too enter an "altered state," but our altered state is different from the one disaster survivors have known: Thanks to the triad of awareness, potential and stillness, our "altered state" does not pass. It is the place we will inhabit forever if we remain committed to living the life of our dreams.

Expanding

When we court clarity, creativity and the joy they bring, our lives begin *expanding* in remarkable ways. Our confidence surges, allowing us to pass beyond a limited comfort zone to discover new territory where we can explore and realize our potential. Opportunities to learn, grow and attain greater success and happiness in life appear naturally, effortlessly and without the quagmire's struggle. Through clarity, creativity and joy we no longer pursue opportunities in painstaking, time-consuming ways. We attract what we want by giving it our life's energy, and we are ready to say, "Yes!" the moment it appears.

A genuine expansion of our lives is not the same as an expansion of a sense of entitlement. In entitlement the individual has relinquished responsibility for her or his life. "The world must take care of me," the entitled feel, and, again, a sense of entitlement often carries with it a posture of victimhood. A genuine expansion of life, on the other hand, demands that we take full responsibility for our lives, that we believe we have the power to make our lives what we wish them to be, and that we refuse ego's whispers of justification for entitlement and victimhood. A sense of entitlement, though it may *feel* freeing to the ego, is not real freedom. It is a child waiting for parents to provide. For an adult, such dependency can only be a prison. When we take responsibility for our lives, with a well-deserved faith in our gifts, we are truly free. The universe has no power over us. We collaborate with the universe to make the lives we want.

When we genuinely expand our lives, others see us (because it is true) as centered, confident and joyous. The stillness at the depth of our being shines through our eyes. We smile with true inner happiness. We express to the universe – both directly and indirectly – how grateful we are for what we have. In our new posture toward life, ourselves and others, what we have is now ours and will help us make the future we desire. How motivated we now are to work effortlessly in the jet stream of ease for what we want! To our amazement people want to spend time with us; companies pursue us; organizations ask for our advice; and out-of-the blue opportunities bloom – because we are living life as everyone would wish to live it if they could, and by doing so we represent hope. Our fellow beings feel grateful.

– Eight –

The Gift of Freedom

Everyone takes the limits of his own vision for the limits of the world.

- Arthur Schopenhauer

When we genuinely use our gifts – those resources within us – we discover a real, awe-inspiring freedom. We awaken to a sense of new power in our lives – to the certainty that in life's epic adventures we have everything we need to excel.

With our exhilaration in the jet stream of ease, we see clearly that the quagmire of negativity – what the human ego has made of the community garden – is merely a reflection of our own state of mind. We see, and without self-recrimination, that our experiences in that quagmire have been a predictable outcome of our own life choices. We see that we can change once and for all the circumstances and old habits of emotion, thought and action that have kept us from the lives we desire and deserve.

Remaking Our Life

By embracing the essential triad of *awareness*, *potential* and *stillness*, we will recognize the circumstances and habits that pull us toward the quagmire. Are we stuck in our basic life-styles – with an unhealthy diet, chronic exhaustion, or lack of exercise? Are we stuck in the unreasonable expectations of others – expectations we've collaborated with? In what ways are we held in the quagmire, or, when we're free of it for a moment, why do we find ourselves returning to it?

In our new life, facing the truth won't always be easy. But if we keep pushing – insisting on seeing clearly and honestly – the moment will come when we understand how to claim our freedom. Liberating ourselves – retrieving ourselves from the quagmire of negativity in order to free our potential – is a process we will complete time and time again. It takes diligence. We will take three steps forward and one step back until our thoughts and emotions become aligned with our new way of being. Even though we are able to ascend to the jet stream of ease, we will, yes, still have our moments in the quagmire; but these moments will teach us what we need to know: Each victory will change our relationship with the quagmire. We will no longer feel trapped when we visit it. Each time we will know the visit is temporary. We will see the quagmire clearly for what it is instead of having ego blind us into thinking the quagmire is all there is.

Choosing to Soar

Freeing ourselves from the quagmire's hold opens us to tremendous opportunity. In our new life we are new people – free to desire, to dream, and to soar in the jet stream of ease. We have crossed freedom's threshold by moving beyond the tangle and immobility of past choices. We have entered an endless sky where the decisions we make based on our new wisdom create a new life of possibility and *complete* satisfaction. Why, then, do we still sometimes hesitate?

Why does the caged bird, its door open, refuse to leave its cage? Does it remain because it simply doesn't realize it's free? Has it grown so accustomed to its environment that it is afraid to leave it? Is it better to be caged in a comfortable prison than risk the unknown, even if the unknown is freedom and joy? The bird may be right, of course: Departing the cage may leave it starving or in the claws of a cat. The human ego doesn't have to worry about starvation or claws, and yet it often prefers comfortable prisons. It will come up with as many excuses as possible to justify its fear and not leave its cage. Yet the ego has even more reason than the bird to follow that open door to freedom – where it can be the creature it has always been, but has somehow forgotten. Still, the ego hesitates, even though there is nothing to fear. And that is what we must tell ourselves constantly at first: How fear is an illusion that will keep us from the joy of living the life of our dreams.

Choosing at last to go for what we want in life opens us up and lets the essential triad of awareness, potential and stillness fill our world with more energy than we ever thought possible. When we truly reach out – using all of our gifts toward our dreams – our inner and outer worlds become free. In that freedom we truly recognize ourselves. We see what life can really be if we'll only leave our cage . . . and *soar*.

Synchronicity

When we choose to embrace the essential triad of awareness, potential and stillness – to remake our life into the one we desire – we "synchronize" with the jet stream. We align the timing of our intentions and actions with a pace of living that flows rather than sputters. Our awareness moves into full glory, and we perceive life on levels we never imagined possible. Cued by hunches – by a knowing at all levels – we begin to rely for our compass on our body as much as our analytical mind; and by doing so we embrace the great speed of the jet stream. Through choosing freedom – and our desire to live in the jet stream of ease – we discover another gift: *synchronicity*, those positive, meaningful coincidences that can help us claim the life we've always wanted. We know we must be the one "attracting" good things – in ways we don't understand, but must instinctively trust – but how are we doing it? We don't need to know. Synchronicity is a by-product of what we are doing correctly. It is the child of our other gifts.

As these meaningful and rewarding coincidences become too frequent to be mere chance, synchronicity itself becomes familiar to us, like a friend. It is as if we have always lived this way. We feel ready for each moment before it occurs. We begin to take synchronicity for granted because this is how life should be and probably was even before, though we could not see it. The negative coincidences of the quagmire – which we were attracting, too, but from ego's posture toward life – have become the beautiful miracles of our new way of living.

With synchronicity now wearing a brighter face in our life, everything becomes possible. We move forward with even greater confidence, joy and power to live from our true potential.

– Nine –

The Gift of Engagement

I had an experience I can't prove, I can't explain it, but everything that I know as a human being, everything that I am tells me that it was real. I was a part of something wonderful, something that changed me forever; a vision of the Universe that tells us undeniably how tiny, and insignificant, and how rare and precious we all are. A vision that tells us we belong to something that is greater than ourselves. That we are not, that none of us, are alone.

- Carl Sagan

As soon as we ask ourselves where our potential might take us, we start to receive answers. All point to the life we have always had the gifts to design, though we didn't know it. In that design we will discover the supreme gift: the gift of authentic *engagement* with the universe and therefore ourselves. We will live life more fully. We will avoid the quagmire's hold, yet learn from its pull. We will not experience loneliness because isolation is an illusion. We will understand that any passivity – toward inner growth or living life fully – must work against our goals.

A completely satisfying life can only come from three actions on our part: (l) Establishing and maintaining a connection to our inner self. (2) Determining to live through awareness, potential, stillness and the many gifts this essential triad provides. (3) Leaving the quagmire of negativity for the jet stream of ease, where the power and method of real engagement can reveal itself.

The quagmire's illusions are ones we once invited into our lives, letting them dictate our perceptions, actions and reactions to life. As we *engage* a larger world beyond the quagmire, we see the enormous role our heart plays in the big picture of life. We discover that the *domain of the heart* is at the very core of life, and that awareness, potential and still-ness flow from that core. We awaken to the truth that each and every experience in life is colored by how engaged our heart is. While life may look gray (or worse) in the quagmire of negativity, it cannot but shine with all the colors of the rainbow in the realm of our hearts and leave us nourished by our wonder at the universe and ourselves.

The Life of Our Dreams

If we live by these nine gifts and their magical children – ones we were born with, but did not see or know how to use – we will make of our life a movie that is right, true, beautiful and well-earned by our commitment. As we watch our life's movie unfold on the universal screen, it will be familiar to us. Why? Because we have always at some level deep within us known how right, true and beautiful it is to answer opportunity's knock and indeed begin living the life of our dreams.

Acknowledgments

I have always strived to live by the age-old wisdom that we must come together to make the world a better place – that anything we can do to help the world and those who live in it is not just "nice," but mandatory. I believe that we must each give in our own way and to the best of our ability. We must support one another in being the best we can be so that we can offer our best to the world. I am most grateful for those who have supported me, through this book, in being my best and offering my best to the world.

The Gifted: How to Live the Life of Your Dreams could not have come into being without the support of my consultant and editor, Bruce McAllister.

Thank you, Bruce, for bringing not only your expertise in writing, but also your passion for and understanding of human potential to this project. Thank you also to my cover designer, Ben McAllister; my graphic designer, Jerry Henness; my marketing expert, Dana Neuts; and my publishing wizard, Bridget McKenna.

In addition, I wish to thank the program participants at the Daphne Michaels Institute for their enthusiastic support of my desire to share my work and message with a greater number of people through this launch of Daphne Michaels Books. The road to realizing this dream would not have been as exhilarating without your encouragement and celebration.

And, finally, to my son Gabriel: Thank you for being such a pure and beautiful teacher and human being. You light up my world.

The Author

Daphne Michaels is an author, speaker and licensed psycho-therapist whose institute has helped hundreds of women and men transform their lives through the "gifts" every human being is born with. Daphne began her own journey of trans-formation at a young age, pursued it fearlessly, and later studied formally in the fields of social science, human services and integral psychology.

The Gifted: How to Live the Life of Your Dreams launches both Daphne Michaels Books and The Gifted series, whose goal it is to share with the widest audience possible the principles that guide the Daphne Michaels Institute. Daphne's earlier book, *Light of Our Times*, featured her conversations with such international figures in the fields of spirituality and personal development as Ram Dass, Julia Cameron, Dr. Masaru Emoto, and Thomas Moore.

Forthcoming Books in The Gifted Series

The Gift of Your Dreams:
How to Make Your Visions Real

The Gift of Charisma:
How to Take Your Life to the Next Level

The Gift of Creativity:
Seven Steps to Extraordinary Living

The Gift of New Sunrises:
How to Partner With Nature for Greater Success

*If you would like pre-publication notifications
of these Daphne Michaels books, please sign up
at www.daphnemichaels.com*

11204299R00077

Made in the USA
San Bernardino, CA
09 May 2014